NO-COOK PALEO!

Quick Eats

Smoothie Recipes

Introduction

This book is for those modern-day cavemen and women following the Paleo style of eating. Eating healthy has never been easier with the variety of colorful, flavorful whole foods that our ancestors survived off of. Who knew you can still enjoy eating while on a diet? Combining fresh fruits, vegetables, nuts, fish and meat provides endless possibilities of delicious recipes. Now, back in the Paleolithic era, there is one tool they were missing and that is the blender. We can now enjoy combinations of vitamin and nutrient-rich whole foods that are packed into an easy to drink smoothie.

Find a collection of smoothie recipes with ingredients that have never been processed or refined. Maximize the health benefits of these foods by supplying your body with a boost of healing power in a variety of flavors. By drinking your nutrients, your body can easily absorb what it needs and have excess energy for body maintenance and activities you choose. With a boost of energy and a satisfied body, watch the pounds melt away by replacing 1 meal a day with a Paleo smoothie. Try the variety of carefully crafted, functional smoothies that are as good for your taste buds as they are for your body.

Table of Contents

Paleo Peach Relief
Morning Melon Smoothie
Paleo Papaya Smoothie
Paleo Lemon Crush
Lime Cooler Crush

Fresh Almond Milk

Prep Time: 5 minutes*

Servings: 2

INGREDIENTS

1 cup raw almonds

4 cups water

INSTRUCTIONS

1. *Soak almonds in 1 cup water at least 6 hours, or overnight.
2. Drain soaked almonds and add to high-speed blender with 3 cups water. Process until well blended and almost smooth, about 1- 2 minutes.
3. Strain mixture through nut milk bag, cheesecloth or strainer into container.
4. Keep refrigerated up to 4 days. If milk separates, mix before use.

Fresh Coconut Milk

Prep Time: 10 minutes

Servings: 2

INGREDIENTS

2 mature coconuts

3 cups water

INSTRUCTIONS

1. Remove flesh from coconuts and add to high-speed blender with 3 cups water. Process until well blended and fairly smooth, about 1-2 minutes.
2. Strain mixture through nut milk bag, cheesecloth or strainer into container.
3. Reserve pulp and set aside to dry and dehydrate, then use as coconut flour.
4. Keep refrigerated up to 4 days. If milk separates, mix before use.

NOTE: Blend additional coconut flesh with prepared coconut milk and strain for thicker coconut milk. Continue blending thickened coconut milk with additional coconut flesh until coconut cream forms. Or set thickened milk aside in refrigerator and allow fat to separate for coconut cream.

Flaked Coconut Milk

Prep Time: 5 minutes*

Servings: 2

INGREDIENTS

2 cups dried coconut (unsweetened shreds or flakes)

4 cups of water

INSTRUCTIONS

1. *Soak dried coconut in 3 cups water at least 6 hours, or overnight in refrigerator.

2. Add soaked coconut and liquid to high-speed blender. Process until well blended and fairly smooth, about 1- 2 minutes. Add extra water for thinner consistency.

3. Strain mixture through nut milk bag, cheesecloth or strainer into container.

4. Reserve pulp and set aside to dry and dehydrate, then use as coconut flour.

5. Keep refrigerated up to 4 days. If milk separates, mix before use.

NOTE: Increase coconut and decrease water for thicker coconut milk. Set thickened milk aside in refrigerator and allow fat to separate for coconut cream.

Primal Green Smoothie

Prep Time: 5 minutes*

Servings: 1

INGREDIENTS

1 cup chopped kale

1/2 cup watercress

1 banana (frozen chunks)

1 green apple

1/2 avocado

1 1/2 cups nut milk (or kefir)

2 - 4 tablespoons sweetener** (optional)

INSTRUCTIONS

1. *Peel banana, then chop and freeze.
2. Remove any stems and ribs from kale. Peel apple if preferred, then core and dice.
3. Slice avocado in half and scoop flesh of pitted half into high-speed blender. Add remaining ingredients and process until smooth, about 1 - 2 minutes.
4. Pour into large glass and serve immediately.

**Stevia, dried dates or raw honey

Green Craving Crush

Prep Time: 5 minutes

Servings: 1

INGREDIENTS

1 cup spinach

1 small zucchini (or 1/2 large)

2 celery stalks

1 cup green grapes

1 1/4 cups nut milk

2 - 4 tablespoons sweetener* (optional)

INSTRUCTIONS

1. Peel zucchini if preferred, then chop. Chop celery stalks.
2. Add all ingredients to high-speed blender. Process until smooth, about 1 - 2 minutes.
3. Pour into large glass and serve immediately.

Stevia, dried dates or raw honey

Primal Spiced Pear Smoothie

Prep Time: 5 minutes*

Servings: 1

INGREDIENTS

2 ripe pears

1 banana (frozen chunks)

1 1/4 cups nut milk

1/2 teaspoon ground cinnamon

1/4 teaspoon ground nutmeg

1/4 teaspoon vanilla

INSTRUCTIONS

1. *Peel banana, then cut into chucks and freeze.
2. Stem and seed pears, then cut into quarters.
3. Add all ingredients to high-speed blender. Process until smooth, about 1 minute.
4. Pour into large glass and serve immediately.

Scarlet Sunrise Smoothie

Prep Time: 5 minutes

Servings: 1

INGREDIENTS

1 cup strawberries (frozen halves)

1/2 cup red raspberries

1/2 cup pitted cherries

1 cup nut milk

1 tablespoon chia or flax seed (optional)

INSTRUCTIONS

1. *Remove stems from strawberries, then cut in half and freeze.
2. Pit cherries, if fresh.
3. Add frozen strawberries and nut milk to high-speed blender. Pulse to break down frozen strawberries.
4. Add remaining ingredients and process until smooth, about 1 minute.
5. Pour into large glass and serve immediately.

Strawberry Banana Smoothie

Prep Time: 5 minutes*

Servings: 1

INGREDIENTS

1 banana (frozen chunks)

1 cup strawberries (frozen halves)

1 1/2 cup nut milk

1/4 teaspoon vanilla

INSTRUCTIONS

1. *Peel banana, then cut into chucks and freeze. Remove stems from strawberries, cut in half and freeze.
2. Add all ingredients to high-speed blender. Process until smooth, about 1- 2 minutes.
3. Pour into large glass and serve immediately.

Primal Piña Colada

Prep Time: 5 minutes*

Servings: 1

INSTRUCTIONS

1 small banana (frozen chunks)

1 cup pineapple (frozen chunks)

1 1/2 cups coconut milk

2 tablespoons flaked coconut (or 1/4 cup fresh coconut)

DIRECTIONS

1. *Peel banana, then cut into chucks and freeze. Peel pineapple, then cut into chunks and freeze.
2. Add all ingredients to high-speed blender. Process until smooth, about 1- 2 minutes.
3. Pour into large glass and serve immediately.

Strawberry Kiwi Slushy

Prep Time: 5 minutes*

Servings: 1

INGREDIENTS

1 cup strawberries (frozen halves)

2 kiwis

1 cup nut milk

1/2 cup orange juice (about 2 oranges)

1 tablespoon chia or flax seed (optional)

INSTRUCTIONS

1. *Remove stems from strawberries, cut in half and freeze.
2. Peel kiwi and cut into quarters. Juice oranges.
3. Add all ingredients to high-speed blender. Process until smooth, about 1- 2 minutes.
4. Pour into large glass and serve immediately.

Carrot Cake Smoothie

Prep Time: 10 minutes*

Servings: 1

INGREDIENTS

1 small banana (frozen chunks)

1/2 cup pineapple (frozen chunks)

2 large carrots

Small piece ginger root

1/2 cup orange juice (about 2 oranges)

1 cup nut milk

1/2 teaspoon ground cinnamon

1 cage-free egg (optional)

INSTRUCTIONS

1. *Peel banana, then cut into chucks and freeze. Peel pineapple, then cut into chunks and freeze.

2. Juice carrots, oranges and ginger root.

3. Add all ingredients to high-speed blender. Process until smooth, about 1- 2 minutes.

4. Pour into large glass and serve immediately.

Cocoa Banana Swirl

Prep Time: 5 minutes

Servings: 1

INGREDIENTS

1 large banana (or 2 small)

2 tablespoons raw cocoa powder

1 cup nut milk

1/2 cup ice

2 - 4 tablespoons sweetener* (optional)

INSTRUCTIONS

1. Peel and chop banana.
2. Add ice and nut milk to high-speed blender. Pulse to crush ice.
3. Add remaining ingredients and process until smooth, about 1- 2 minutes.
4. Pour into large glass and serve immediately.

*Stevia, dried dates or raw honey

Cucumber Melon Smoothie

Prep Time: 5 minutes*

Servings: 2

INGREDIENTS

1 small cucumber

1 cup watermelon (chunks)

1 cup honeydew melon (frozen chunks)

1 cup coconut milk

2 - 4 tablespoons sweetener** (optional)

INSTRUCTIONS

1. * Cut honeydew flesh away from peel, then cut into chunks and freeze.
2. Peel cucumber and remove seeds, then cut into chunks. Cut watermelon flesh away from rind, then remove seeds and cut into chunks.
3. Add all ingredients to high-speed blender. Process until smooth, about 1 minute.
4. Pour into large glasses and serve immediately.

**Stevia, dried dates or raw honey*

Super Strawberry Smoothie

Prep Time: 5 minutes*

Servings: 1

INGREDIENTS

1 cup strawberries

1 cup strawberries (frozen halves)

2 cups coconut milk

1/2 teaspoon vanilla

2 tablespoons chia or flax seed (optional)

INSTRUCTIONS

1. * Remove stems from 1 cup strawberries, then cut in half and freeze.
2. Remove stems from 1 cup fresh strawberries.
3. Add frozen strawberries and coconut milk to high-speed blender. Pulse to break down frozen strawberries.
4. Add remaining ingredients and process until smooth, about 1- 2 minutes.
5. Pour into large glass and serve immediately.

Banana Berry Smoothie

Prep Time: 5 minutes*

Servings: 1

INGREDIENTS

1 banana (frozen chunks)

1/2 cup strawberries (frozen halves)

1/4 cup blueberries

1/4 cup blackberries

1 1/2 cups nut milk

1/2 teaspoon vanilla

2 tablespoons chia or flax seed (optional)

INSTRUCTIONS

1. *Peel banana, then cut into chucks and freeze. Remove stems from strawberries, then cut in half and freeze.
2. Add all ingredients to high-speed blender. Process until smooth, about 1 - 2 minutes.
3. Pour into large glass and serve immediately.

Blue Sky Berry Smoothie

Prep Time: 5 minutes

Servings: 1

INGREDIENTS

1 cup blueberries (frozen)

1/4 cup black raspberries

1/4 cup blackberries

1/4 cup pitted black cherries

1 /2 cups nut milk

1/2 teaspoon vanilla

2 tablespoons chia or flax seed (optional)

INSTRUCTIONS

1. *Freeze blueberries.
2. Add alls ingredients to high-speed blender. Process until smooth, about 1 minute.
3. Pour into large glass and serve immediately.

Nutter Butter Shake

Prep Time: 5 minutes*

Servings: 1

INGREDIENTS

1 banana (frozen chunks)

1/4 cup raw almond butter (or 1/2 cup raw almonds)

1 cup nut milk

2 - 4 tablespoons sweetener**

INSTRUCTIONS

1. *Peel banana, then cut into chucks and freeze.
2. Add raw almonds to food processor or high speed blender and process until smooth, about 3 minutes. Or use prepared raw almond butter.
3. Add all ingredients to high-speed blender. Process until smooth, about 1 - 2 minutes.
4. Pour into large glass and serve immediately.

**Stevia, dried dates or raw honey*

Primal Sunrise Orange Smoothie

Prep Time: 5 minutes

Servings: 1

INGREDIENTS

1 1/2 cups orange or tangerine juice (about 6 oranges or 10 tangerines)

1/2 cup coconut cream (or thick coconut milk)

2/3 cup ice

1 cage-free egg (optional)

2 tablespoons sweetener* (optional)

INSTRUCTIONS

1. Juice oranges.
2. Add ice and orange juice to high-speed blender. Pulse to crush ice.
3. Add remaining ingredients and process until smooth, about 1 minute.
4. Pour into large glass and serve immediately.

Stevia, dried dates or raw honey

Paleo Mango Smoothie

Prep Time: 5 minutes

Servings: 1

INGREDIENTS

1 ripe mango

1 cup coconut milk

1/2 cup ice

1 cage-free egg (optional)

2 - 4 tablespoons sweetener* (optional)

INSTRUCTIONS

1. Cut flesh of mango from pit. Remove peel and cut into chunks.
2. Add ice and coconut milk to high-speed blender. Pulse to crush ice.
3. Add remaining ingredients and process until smooth, about 1 minute.
4. Pour into large glass and serve immediately.

Stevia, dried dates or raw honey

Mongolian Morning Smoothie

Prep Time: 5 minutes*

Servings: 1

INGREDIENTS

1 cup strawberries

1/2 cup strawberries (frozen halves)

1 cup orange juice (about 4 oranges)

1/2 cup thick coconut milk (or kefir)

2 tablespoons chia or flax seed (optional)

INSTRUCTIONS

1. *Remove stems from 1/2 cup strawberries, then cut in half and freeze.
2. Remove stem from fresh strawberries. Juice oranges
3. Add frozen strawberries and orange juice to high-speed blender. Pulse to break down frozen strawberries.
4. Add remaining ingredients and process until smooth, about 1 minute.
5. Pour into large glass and serve immediately.

Chocolate Avocado Shake

Prep Time: 5 minutes

Servings: 1

INGREDIENTS

1 ripe avocado

1 cup coconut milk (or kefir)

1/3 cup ice

1/2 teaspoon vanilla

2 - 4 tablespoons sweetener*

2 tablespoons raw cocoa powder (optional)

INSTRUCTIONS

1. Add ice and coconut milk to high-speed blender. Pulse to crush ice.
2. Slice avocado in half and remove pit. Scoop into high-speed blender.
3. Add remaining ingredients and process until smooth, about 1 minute.
4. Pour into large glass and serve immediately.

*Stevia, dried dates or raw honey

Sweet Watermelon Slushy

Prep Time: 5 minutes*

Servings: 1

INGREDIENTS

2 cups watermelon (chunks)

1/2 cup strawberries (frozen halves)

2 limes

1/2 cup thick coconut milk

2 - 4 tablespoons sweetener**

INSTRUCTIONS

1. *Remove stems from strawberries, then cut in halve and freeze.
2. Cut watermelon flesh away from rind and cut into chunks. Juice limes.
3. Add frozen strawberries, lime juice and nut milk to high-speed blender. Pulse to break down frozen strawberries.
4. Add all ingredients and to high-speed blender. process until smooth, about 1 minute.
5. Pour into large glass and serve immediately.

**Stevia, dried dates or raw honey*

Bananarama Shake

Prep Time: 5 minutes*

Servings: 1

INGREDIENTS

1 banana (frozen chunks)

1 plum

1/4 cup pitted prunes

1 cup nut milk

1/2 cup orange juice (about 2 oranges)

1 cage-free egg (optional)

INSTRUCTIONS

1. *Peel banana, then cut into chucks and freeze.
2. Cut plum in half and remove pit, then quarter. Juice oranges.
3. Add all ingredients to high-speed blender. Process until smooth, about 1 - 2 minutes.
4. Pour into large glass and serve immediately.

Paleo Peach Relief

Prep Time: 5 minutes

Servings: 1

INGREDIENTS

1 ripe peach or nectarine (frozen chunks)

2 fresh apricots (or 1/4 cup dried)

1/2 cup nut milk (or kefir)

1/2 cup fresh orange juice (about 2 oranges)

1 cage-free egg (optional)

INSTRUCTIONS

1. *Cut peach in half and remove pit, then cut into chucks and freeze.
2. Cut fresh apricots in half and remove pits, then cut into chucks, if using. Juice oranges.
3. Add all ingredients to high-speed blender. Process until smooth, about 1 minute.
4. Pour into large glass and serve immediately.

Morning Melon Smoothie

Prep Time: 5 minutes*

Servings: 1

INGREDIENTS

1 cup honeydew melon (frozen chunks)

1 cup cantaloupe (chunks)

1 grapefruit (about 2/3 cup juice)

2/3 cup thick coconut milk

2 - 4 tablespoons sweetener**

INSTRUCTIONS

1. *Cut honeydew melon flesh away from rind, then cut into chunks and freeze.
2. Cut cantaloupe flesh away from rind, then cut into chunks. Juice grapefruit.
3. Add frozen honeydew chunks and grapefruit juice to high-speed blender. Pulse to break down frozen honeydew.
4. Add remaining ingredients and process until smooth, about 1 minute.
5. Pour into large glass and serve immediately.

**Stevia, dried dates or raw honey*

Paleo Papaya Smoothie

Prep Time: 5 minutes

Servings: 1

INGREDIENTS

1 mango (frozen chunks)

1/2 cup papaya (chunks)

1 ripe guava

2 limes

1 cup coconut milk

INSTRUCTIONS

1. *Cut mango flesh away from pit and peel. Then dice into small chunks and freeze.
2. Peel papaya and remove seeds, then cut into chunks. Peel guava if preferred, then cut in half. Juice limes.
3. Add coconut milk and guava to high-speed blender. Process until smooth. Strain out seeds, reserving liquid.
4. Add strained guava mixture back to high-speed blender with frozen mango chunks. Pulse to break down frozen mango.
5. Add remaining ingredients and process until smooth, about 1 minute.
6. Pour into large glass and serve immediately.

Paleo Lemon Crush

Prep Time: 5 minutes

Servings: 1

INGREDIENTS

1/2 cup fresh lemon juice (about 3 lemons)

1/2 cup fresh orange juice (about 2 oranges)

1/2 cup coconut milk

1/2 cup ice

2 - 4 tablespoons sweetener*

INSTRUCTIONS

1. Juice lemons and oranges.
2. Add ice and coconut milk to high-speed blender. Pulse to crush ice.
3. Add remaining ingredients and process until smooth, about 1 minute.
4. Pour into large glass and serve immediately.

*Stevia, dried dates or raw honey

Lime Cooler Crush

Prep Time: 5 minutes

Servings: 1

INGREDIENTS

1/2 cup lime juice (about 5 limes)

1 sprig fresh mint

1/2 cup thick coconut milk

2 tablespoons flaked coconut (or 1/4 cup fresh coconut)

1/2 cup ice

2 - 4 tablespoons sweetener*

1/2 teaspoon vanilla (optional)

INSTRUCTIONS

1. Remove mint leaves from stem. Juice limes.
2. Add ice and limes juice to high-speed blender. Pulse to crush ice.
3. Add remaining ingredients to high-speed blender and process until smooth, about 1 minute.
4. Pour into large glass and serve immediately.

Stevia, dried dates or raw honey

Dessert Recipes

Introduction

No cave bound, club wielding, hair dragging people here. Contrary to popular rumor, the Paleo way of eating is about health. Let's first say that all of the hoopla about some cave diet is just a bunch of hooey! The Paleo way of eating is simply put, a natural and healthy style of eating. Many people figure that because the Paleo style of eating limits ingredient usage that good meal ideas are hard to come by.

All kidding aside, this book was designed to make all of your friends and family think that you have Paleo super powers.

In his cook book – or shall I say cave-scripture, you will find tons of all natural, no-cooking-required, totally Paleo friendly recipes that will help you towards your health improvement goals!

Table of Contents

Paleo Plains Banana Bread

Moist Coconut Macaroons

Delicious Chocolate Chip Cookies

All-American Almond Biscotti

Simple Ginger Pudding

Primal Strawberry Ice Cream

Coconut Mango Sorbet

Paleo Banana Pie

Prep Time: 10 minutes*

Servings: 8

INGREDIENTS

Crust

1 cup raw cashews

1 cup flaked or shredded coconut

1/2 cup dried pitted dates

1/4 teaspoon vanilla

1/4 teaspoon Celtic sea salt

Banana Filling

2 ripe bananas

3/4 cup raw cashews (or 1/2 cup raw cashew butter)

1/3 cup raw coconut oil (or raw coconut or cacao butter, melted)

1/4 cup raw honey (or dried pitted dates, soaked overnight)

Juice of 2 lemons

1 teaspoon vanilla

Pinch Celtic sea salt

Water (optional)

INSTRUCTIONS

1. *For *Banana Filling*, soak dates in enough water to cover overnight in refrigerator, if using. Drain.

2. For *Crust*, place all ingredients in food processor or high-speed blender. Process until well ground and mixture sticks together, about 1 - 2 minutes.

3. Press *Crust* firmly into pie plate, cake pan or baking dish with hands.

4. For *Banana Filling*, peel bananas and juice lemons. Add to clean food processor or high-speed blender with cashews or cashew butter, coconut oil or butter, vanilla, salt and honey or soaked dates. Process until creamy and smooth, about 1 - 2 minutes.

5. Pour *Banana Filling* into *Crust* and smooth with spatula or back of a spoon.

6. *Cover pie with parchment, if preferred, and place in freezer at least 8 hours, or overnight.

7. Slice and serve chilled. Or allow to soften slightly, then serve. Store leftovers in freezer.

Chocolate Cream Pie

Prep Time: 15 minutes*

Servings: 8

INGREDIENTS

Crust

1 cup dried pitted dates

3/4 cup raw almonds

1/2 cup raw walnuts

3 tablespoons raw cocoa powder

1/2 teaspoon vanilla

1/4 teaspoon Celtic sea salt

Water

Chocolate Cream Filling

4 cups raw cashews

1/2 cup raw honey (or 1 cup dried pitted dates)

1/4 cup raw cocoa powder

3 teaspoons vanilla

2 tablespoons cacao nibs (or raw chocolate chips or raw chocolate bark)

Water

INSTRUCTIONS

1. *For *Crust*, soak dates in enough water to cover for 1 hour, then drain.

2. *For *Chocolate Cream Filling*, soak cashews in enough water to cover overnight in refrigerator. Drain and rinse. Set aside. Soak

dates in enough water to cover overnight in refrigerator, if using. Drain, reserving soaking liquid.

3. For *Crust*, place all ingredients in food processor or high-speed blender. Process until well ground and mixture sticks together, about 2 minutes.

4. Press *Crust* firmly into pie plate, cake pan or baking dish with hands. Set aside in refrigerator or freezer, if preferred.

5. For *Chocolate Cream Filling*, add soaked cashews, vanilla, and dates or honey to clean food processor or high-speed blender. Process until smooth, about 2 minutes. Add enough date soaking liquid or water to reach desired consistency. Mixture should be thick and smooth, but not runny.

6. Transfer half of mixture to small mixing bowl and set aside. Add cocoa to processor and process until incorporated.

7. Pour *Chocolate Cream Filling* into *Crust* and smooth with spatula or back of a spoon. Top with reserved *Cream Filling* and smooth with spatula or back of a spoon. Chop cacao nibs, or shave chocolate bark. Sprinkle chopped nibs, chocolate shaving or chocolate chips over pie.

8. *Refrigerate or freeze at least 1 hour, until set. Slice and serve chilled.

Sweet Lemon Cheesecake

Prep Time: 15 minutes*

Servings: 8

INGREDIENTS

Crust

2 cups raw almonds

1/2 cup dried pitted dates

1/4 cup flaked or shredded coconut

Lemon Cheesecake Filling

3 cups raw cashews

3/4 cup fresh lemon juice (about 6 lemons)

3/4 cup raw honey (or 1 cup dried pitted dates)

3/4 cup raw coconut oil (or raw coconut or cacao butter, melted)

1 teaspoon vanilla

1/2 teaspoon Celtic sea salt

INSTRUCTIONS

1. *For *Crust*, soak almonds in enough water to cover overnight in refrigerator. Drain and rinse.

2. *For *Lemon Cheesecake Filling*, soak cashews in enough water to cover for 4 hours. Drain and rinse. Set aside. Soak dates in enough water to cover overnight in refrigerator, if using. Drain, reserving soaking liquid.

3. For *Crust*, place all ingredients in food processor or high-speed blender. Process until well ground and mixture sticks together, about 2 minutes.

4. Press *Crust* firmly into pie plate, cake pan or baking dish with hands. Set aside in refrigerator or freezer, if preferred.

5. For *Lemon Cheesecake Filling*, zest 1 lemon, then juice all lemons into clean food processor or high-speed blender. Add soaked cashews, vanilla, coconut oil or butter, salt, and honey or dates to clean food processor or high-speed blender. Process until smooth, about 2 - 3 minutes. Add enough date soaking liquid or water to reach desired consistency, if necessary. Mixture should be thick and smooth, but not runny.

6. Pour *Lemon Cheesecake Filling* into *Crust* and gently tap dish on counter to release any air bubbles. Smooth with spatula or back of a spoon, if needed.

7. *Cover pie with parchment, if preferred, and place in freezer at least 3 hours. Allow to warm slightly and serve chilled.

Primal Key Lime Pie

Prep Time: 15 minutes*

Servings: 8

INGREDIENTS

Crust

1 cup raw macadamia nuts

1 cup raw cashews

1/3 cup flaked or shredded coconut

1/4 cup dried pitted dates

1 teaspoon vanilla

1/2 teaspoon Celtic sea salt

Key Lime Filling

1 1/2 cups raw cashews

1 ripe avocado

3/4 cup key lime juice (about 8 key limes)

3/4 cup raw honey (or 1cup dried pitted dates)

1/4 cup raw coconut oil (or raw coconut or cacao butter, melted)

1 tablespoon vanilla

1/4 teaspoon Celtic sea salt

1/2 teaspoon spirulina or spinach powder (optional)

INSTRUCTIONS

1. *For *Key Lime Filling*, soak cashews in enough water to cover for 1 hour. Drain and rinse. Set aside. Soak dates in enough water to

cover overnight in refrigerator, if using. Drain, reserving soaking liquid.

2. For *Crust*, place all ingredients in food processor or high-speed blender. Process until well ground and mixture sticks together, about 2 minutes.

3. Press *Crust* firmly into pie plate, cake pan or baking dish with hands. Set aside in refrigerator or freezer, if preferred.

4. For *Key Lime Filling*, zest 1 lime, then juice all limes into clean food processor or high-speed blender. Cut avocado in half and scoop flesh into processor.

5. Add soaked cashews, coconut oil or butter, honey or soaked dates, vanilla, salt and spirulina and spinach powder (optional). Process until smooth, about 2 - 3 minutes. Add enough date soaking liquid or water to reach desired consistency, if necessary. Mixture should be thick and smooth, but not runny.

6. Pour *Key Lime Filling* into *Crust* and gently tap dish on counter to release any air bubbles. Smooth with spatula or back of a spoon, if needed.

7. *Cover pie with parchment, if preferred, and place in freezer at least 3 hours. Allow to warm slightly and serve chilled.

Paleo Coconut Cream Pie

Prep Time: 20 minutes*

Servings: 8

INGREDIENTS

Crust

3/4 cup raw macadamia nuts

3/4 cup raw almonds

1/2 cup dried pitted dates

1/2 cup flaked or shredded coconut

Coconut Cream Filling

1 1/2 cups raw cashews

1 1/2 cups flaked or shredded coconut

3/4 cup raw honey (or 1 cup dried pitted dates))

3/4 cup raw coconut oil (or coconut or cacao butter, melted)

1 teaspoon vanilla

1/2 teaspoon Celtic sea salt

Water

INSTRUCTIONS

1. *For *Crust*, soak almonds in enough water to cover overnight in refrigerator. Drain and rinse.

2. *For *Coconut Cream Filling*, soak cashews in enough water to cover for 4 hours. Drain and rinse. Set aside. Soak coconut in 2 cups water overnight in refrigerator. Drain, reserving soaking

liquid. Soak dates in enough water to cover overnight in refrigerator, if using. Drain, reserving soaking liquid.

3. For *Crust*, place all ingredients in food processor or high-speed blender. Process until well ground and mixture sticks together, about 2 minutes.

4. Press *Crust* firmly into pie plate, cake pan or baking dish with hands. Set aside in refrigerator or freezer, if preferred.

1. For *Coconut Cream Filling*, add soaked coconut to clean food processor or high-speed blender. Process until smooth and creamy, up to 5 minutes. Scrape down sides of bowl as necessary.

5. Add soaked cashews, vanilla, coconut oil or butter, salt, and honey or dates to processor. Process until smooth, about 2 - 3 minutes. Add enough date and/or coconut soaking liquid or water to reach desired constancy, if necessary. Mixture should be thick and smooth, but not runny.

6. Pour *Coconut Cream Filling* into *Crust* and gently tap dish on the counter to release any air bubbles. Smooth with spatula or back of a spoon, if needed.

7. *Cover pie with parchment, if preferred, and place in freezer at least 3 hours. Allow to warm slightly and serve chilled.

Primal Pecan Pie

Prep Time: 15 minutes*

Servings: 8

INGREDIENTS

Crust

3/4 cup raw pecans

3/4 cup raw walnuts

1 1/4 cups dried pitted dates

1/4 cup flaked or shredded coconut

1/4 teaspoon Celtic sea salt

Pecan Filling

1 2/3 cups dried pitted dates

1/2 raw pecan pieces (or 3/4 raw pecan halves)

3/4 cup raw pecan halves (reserve)

1/4 cup raw coconut oil (or raw coconut or cacao butter, melted)

1 1/2 teaspoons vanilla

1 teaspoon ground cinnamon

1/4 teaspoon ground nutmeg

1/2 teaspoon Celtic sea salt

Water

INSTRUCTIONS

1. *For *Pecan Filling,* soak dates in enough water to cover for at least 4 hours, or overnight in refrigerator. Drain, reserving soaking liquid .

2. For *Crust*, place all ingredients in food processor or high-speed blender. Process until mixture is well ground and sticks together, about 2 - 3 minutes.

3. Press *Crust* firmly into pie plate, cake pan or baking dish with hands. Set aside in refrigerator or freezer, if preferred.

4. For *Pecan Filling*, add soaked dates to clean food processor or high-speed blender with pecan pieces, coconut oil or butter, vanilla, salt and spices. Process until thick smooth mixture forms, about 2 - 3 minutes. Add enough soaking liquid to reach desired consistency.

5. Pour *Pecan Filling* into *Crust* and smooth with spatula or back of a spoon. Top pie with reserve pecan halves.

6. Slice and serve immediately. Or refrigerate at least 1 hour and serve chilled.

Simple Mince Pie

Prep Time: 15 minutes*

Servings: 8

INGREDIENTS

Crust

1 cup raw almonds

1 cup raw pecans

1 cup raw walnuts

1 1/2 cups dried pitted dates

1/2 orange

1/2 teaspoon vanilla

1/2 teaspoon ground cinnamon

1/4 teaspoon ground nutmeg

1/4 teaspoon Celtic sea salt

Mincemeat Filling

2 cups dried pitted dates

1/2 cup raw almonds

1/2 cup dried apricots

1 1/2 oranges

1/2 lemon

2 tablespoons raw tahini

2 tablespoons raisins

2 tablespoons dried cherries (or goji or noni berries)

2 tablespoons raw pistachios

2 tablespoons shredded or flaked coconut

1 tablespoon chia seeds

1 teaspoon vanilla

1 teaspoon ground cinnamon

1/4 teaspoon ground nutmeg

1/4 teaspoon ground ginger

1/4 teaspoon Celtic sea salt

Water

INSTRUCTIONS

1. *For *Mincemeat Filling,* soak dates in enough water to cover for 1 hour, then drain.

2. For *Crust*, zest then juice orange into food processor or high-speed blender. Add all *Crust* ingredients and process until well ground and mixture sticks together, about 2 - 3 minutes.

3. Press *Crust* firmly into pie plate, cake pan or baking dish with hands. Set aside in refrigerator or freezer, if preferred.

4. For *Mincemeat Filling*, add chia to clean food processor or high-speed blender and process until finely ground, about 1 minute. Add raw almonds and process until finely ground, about 2 minutes.

5. Zest *then* juice oranges and lemon. Add to processor with soaked dates, tahini, salt and spices. Process until well ground and fairly smooth, about 2 minutes. Add apricots and pulse until roughly chopped.

6. Transfer to medium mixing bowl and stir in raisins and cherries. Mix to combine.

7. Pour *Mincemeat Filling* into *Crust* and smooth with spatula or back of a spoon. Roughly chop pistachios. Sprinkle chopped pistachios and coconut over pie.

8. Slice and serve immediately. Or refrigerate at least 1 hour and serve chilled.

Pumpkin Spice Pie

Prep Time: 15 minutes*

Servings: 8

INGREDIENTS

Crust

3/4 cup raw pecans

3/4 cup raw walnuts

1 1/4 cups dried pitted dates

Pinch Celtic sea salt

Pumpkin Filling

1 "pie pumpkin"

1 1/2 cups dried pitted dates

1/2 cup dried apricots

2 teaspoons ground cinnamon

1/2 teaspoon ground ginger

1/2 teaspoon vanilla

Water

INSTRUCTIONS

1. *For *Crust*, soak dates in enough water to cover for 1 hour, then drain.

2. *For *Pumpkin Filling,* soak dates in enough water to cover for at least 4 hours, or overnight in refrigerator. Drain, reserving soaking liquid .

3. For *Crust*, place all ingredients in food processor or high-speed blender. Process until mixture is well ground and sticks together, about 2 - 3 minutes.

4. Press *Crust* firmly into pie plate, cake pan or baking dish with hands. Set aside in refrigerator or freezer, if preferred.

5. For *Pumpkin Filling*, peel pumpkin and remove seeds and stringy innards. Chop pumpkin and add to clean food processor or high-speed blender with soaked dates, apricots, vanilla, cinnamon and ginger. Process until smooth, up to 5 minutes. Add enough soaking liquid to reach desired consistency. Mixture should be thick and smooth, but not runny.

6. Pour *Pumpkin Filling* into *Crust* and smooth with spatula or back of a spoon.

7. Slice and serve immediately. Or refrigerate at least 1 hour and serve chilled.

Paleo Strawberry Cream Pie

Prep Time: 15 minutes*

Servings: 8

INGREDIENTS

Crust

1 cup raw macadamia nuts

1/2 cup raw walnuts

1/2 cup dried pitted dates

1/4 cup flaked or shredded coconut

Strawberry Cheesecake Filling

2 1/2 cups raw cashews

2 cups strawberries (fresh or thawed)

1/2 cup raw honey (or dried pitted dates)

1/2 cup raw coconut oil (or raw coconut or cacao butter, melted)

1 teaspoon vanilla

INSTRUCTIONS

8. *For *Strawberry Cheesecake Filling*, soak cashews in enough water to cover for 4 hours. Drain and rinse. Set aside. Soak dates in enough water to cover overnight in refrigerator, if using. Drain, reserving soaking liquid.

9. For *Crust*, place all ingredients in food processor or high-speed blender. Process until well ground and mixture sticks together, about 2 minutes.

10. Press *Crust* firmly into pie plate, cake pan or baking dish with hands. Set aside in refrigerator or freezer, if preferred.

11. For *Strawberry Cheesecake Filling*, remove stems from fresh strawberries, or thaw frozen strawberries. Add to clean food processor or high-speed blender with soaked cashews, honey or soaked dates, coconut oil or butter, and vanilla. Process until smooth, about 2 - 3 minutes. Add enough date soaking liquid or water to reach desired consistency, if necessary. Mixture should be thick and smooth, but not runny.

12. Pour *Strawberry Cheesecake Filling* into *Crust* and gently tap dish on counter to release any air bubbles. Smooth with spatula or back of a spoon, if needed.

13. *Cover pie with parchment, if preferred, and place in freezer at least 2 hours. Allow to warm slightly and serve chilled.

Primal Lemon Curd Tart

Prep Time: 10 minutes*

Servings: 8

INGREDIENTS

1 1/2 cups fresh blueberries

Tart Shell

1 cup raw cashews (or raw walnuts)

1 cup raw macadamia nuts (or raw brazil nuts)

1/3 cup flaked or shredded coconut

1 cup dried pitted dates

1/2 teaspoon vanilla

Lemon Curd Filling

1 cup cashews

1/2 cup raw coconut butter (or raw cacao butter)

4 lemons

1/3 - 1/2 cup raw honey (or dried pitted dates)

Pinch Celtic sea salt

Pinch vanilla (optional)

Pinch ground turmeric (optional)

Water

INSTRUCTIONS

8. *For *Lemon Curd Filling*, soak cashews in enough water to cover at least 4 hours, or overnight in refrigerator. Drain and rinse. Set

aside. Soak dates in enough water to cover overnight in refrigerator, if using. Drain, reserving soaking liquid.

1. For *Tart Shell*, place all ingredients in food processor or high-speed blender. Process until well ground and mixture sticks together, about 2 minutes.

2. Press *Crust* firmly into tart pan or pie plate with hands. Set aside in refrigerator or freezer, if preferred.

3. For *Lemon Curd Filling*, zest 1 lemon, then juice all lemons into clean food processor or high-speed blender. Add soaked cashews, soaked dates or honey, salt, and vanilla and turmeric (optional). Process until smooth, about 2 minutes. Add enough soaking liquid or water to reach desired consistency. Mixture should be smooth, but not too runny.

4. Pour *Lemon Curd Filling* into *Crust* and smooth with spatula or back of a spoon. Tp pie with fresh blueberries.

5. Refrigerate at least 1 hour, until set. Slice and serve chilled

Tangy Apricot Tart

Prep Time: 10 minutes*

Servings: 8

INGREDIENTS

Crust

1 cup raw cashews

1 cup raw macadamia nuts (or raw brazil nuts)

1/3 cup flaked or shredded coconut

1 cup dried pitted dates

1/2 teaspoon vanilla

Apricot Filling

3 cups dried apricots

1/2 lemon

Water

INSTRUCTIONS

1. *For *Apricot Filling*, soak 2 1/2 cups apricots in enough water to cover for 2 hours. Drain, reserving soaking liquid.
2. For *Crust*, place all ingredients in food processor or high-speed blender. Process until well ground and mixture sticks together, about 2 minutes.
3. Press *Crust* firmly into pie plate, cake pan or baking dish with hands. Set aside in refrigerator or freezer, if preferred.
4. For *Apricot Filling*, zest then juice lemon into clean food processor or high-speed blender. Add soaked apricots and process until

smooth, about 1 - 2 minutes. Add enough soaking liquid to reach desired consistency. Mixture should be thick and smooth, but not runny.

5. Pour *Apricot Filling* into *Crust* and smooth with spatula or back of a spoon. Chop remaining unsoaked apricots and sprinkle over pie.

6. Slice and serve immediately. Or refrigerate at least 1 hour and serve chilled.

Easy Peasy Apple Pie

Prep Time: 25 minutes*

Servings: 8

INGREDIENTS

Topping

1/2 cup raw pecans

1/2 cup raw walnuts

1/2 cup raw almonds

Crust

1 cup raw almonds

1 cup raw pecans

1 cup raw walnuts

1 1/2 cups dried pitted dates

1 teaspoon vanilla

1/2 teaspoon ground cinnamon

1/2 teaspoon Celtic sea salt

Apple Filling

3 apples

1/4 - 1/3 cup dried pitted dates

1/2 lemon

2 tablespoons flax seeds

1 teaspoon vanilla

1 teaspoon ground cinnamon

1/2 teaspoon Celtic sea salt

Water

INSTRUCTIONS

1. *For Apple Filling*, soak dates in enough water to cover for 1 hour, then drain.

2. For *Topping*, add nuts to food processor or high-speed blender. Pulse until finely chopped. Set aside.

3. For *Crust*, place all ingredients in food processor or high-speed blender. Process until well ground and mixture sticks together, about 2 - 3 minutes.

4. Press *Crust* firmly into pie plate, cake pan or baking dish with hands. Set aside in refrigerator or freezer, if preferred.

5. For *Apple Filling*, add flax to clean food processor or high-speed blender and process until finely ground, about 1 minute.

6. Peel and core apples, then roughly chop. Juice lemon and add to processor with 1/3 of apples, soaked dates, vanilla and salt. Process until smooth, about 2 minutes.

7. Add 1/2 of remaining apples and process until finely chopped, but still chunky. Add remaining apples and pulse until roughly chopped. Set aside 15 minutes.

8. Pour *Apple Filling* into *Crust* and smooth with spatula or back of a spoon. Evenly sprinkle *Topping* over pie to create top crust.

9. Slice and serve immediately. Or refrigerate at least 1 hour and serve chilled.

Peach Pie Perfection

Prep Time: 10 minutes*

Servings: 8

INGREDIENTS

Crust

1 cup raw pecans

1 cup raw walnuts

1 cup dried pitted dates

1/2 teaspoon vanilla

1/2 teaspoon ground cinnamon

1/4 teaspoon Celtic sea salt

Peach Filling

4 ripe peaches (or nectarines)

1 teaspoon ground cinnamon

1/2 teaspoon ground nutmeg

1/4 teaspoon vanilla

1/4 teaspoon ground ginger (optional)

INSTRUCTIONS

10. For *Crust*, place all ingredients in food processor or high-speed blender. Process until well ground and mixture sticks together, about 2 minutes.

11. Press *Crust* firmly into pie plate, cake pan or baking dish with hands. Set aside in refrigerator or freezer, if preferred.

12. For *Peach Filling*, cut peaches in half and remove pit. Thinly slice and add to large mixing bowl. Sprinkle on spices and salt. Gently toss to coat evenly.

13. Pour *Peach Filling* and press into *Crust*.

14. Slice and serve immediately. Or refrigerate at least 1 hour and serve chilled.

Primal Cherry Pie

Prep Time: 15 minutes*

Servings: 8

INGREDIENTS

Crust

1 1/2 cups raw hazelnuts (or macadamia nuts)

1 cup raw almonds

1/4 cup dried pitted dates

1 teaspoon ground cinnamon

Blueberry Filling

4 cups pitted cherries (fresh or thawed)

1/4 cup raw coconut oil (or raw coconut or cacao butter, melted)

1/4 dried pitted dates

1/2 teaspoon vanilla

Pinch Celtic sea salt

INSTRUCTIONS

1. *For *Crust*, soak dates in enough water to cover for 1 hour, then drain.
2. Add nuts to food processor or high-speed blender and process until coarsely ground, about 1 minute. Add dates and cinnamon and process until mixture is well ground and sticks together, about 1 minute.
3. Press *Crust* firmly into pie plate, cake pan or baking dish with hands. Set aside in refrigerator or freezer, if preferred.

4. *For *Cherry Filling*, pit whole cherries, if using.

5. Add 1/3 of pitted cherries to clean food processor or high-speed blender with coconut oil or butter, dates, vanilla and salt. Process until smooth, about 1 - 2 minutes.

6. Add 1/2 of remaining cherries to processor and pulse to roughly chop.

7. Pour *Cherry Filling* into *Crust* and smooth with spatula or back of a spoon. Roughly chop or halve remaining cherries. Sprinkle remaining cherries over pie.

8. *Refrigerate at least 1 hour, until set. Slice and serve chilled. Or allow to warm slightly and serve.

Blueberry Pie

Prep Time: 15 minutes*

Servings: 8

INGREDIENTS

Crust

1 cup raw almonds (or raw pecans)

1 cup dried pitted dates

1 1/2 cups flaked or shredded coconut

1/2 lemon

1 teaspoon vanilla

Pinch Celtic sea salt

Blueberry Filling

2 cups blueberries (fresh or thawed)

1/2 cup raw coconut oil (or raw coconut or cacao butter, melted)

1/4 cup cashew butter(or 1/2 cup raw cashews)

1/4 - 1/3 cup dried pitted dates

1/2 lemon

1 teaspoon vanilla

1/4 teaspoon Celtic sea salt

INSTRUCTIONS

1. For *Crust*, add almonds to food processor or high-speed blender and process until finely ground, about 2 minutes. Zest *then* juice lemon in to processer with remaining *Crust* ingredients. Process until mixture is well ground and sticks together, about 2 minutes.

2. Press *Crust* firmly into pie plate, cake pan or baking dish with hands. Set aside in refrigerator or freezer, if preferred.

3. For *Blueberry Filling*, zest *then* juice lemon into clean food processor or high-speed blender. Add raw cashews and blend until smooth, if using.

4. Or add cashew butter, dates, and coconut oil or butter to processor. Process until smooth, about 1 - 2 minutes.

5. Add 1 1/2 cups blueberries, vanilla and salt to processor. Process until thick smooth mixture forms, about 1 minute.

6. Pour *Blueberry Filling* into *Crust* and smooth with spatula or back of a spoon. Sprinkle remaining blueberries over pie.

7. Slice and serve immediately. Or refrigerate at least 1 hour and serve chilled.

Ice Box Carrot Cake

Prep Time: 10 minutes*

Servings: 8

INGREDIENTS

Carrot Cake

2 - 3 large carrots

2 cups raw walnuts

1/2 cup raisins (or dried apricots)

1/2 cup flaked or shredded coconut

2 tablespoons raw pumpkin seeds

1/4 cup raw honey (or dried pitted dates)

1 teaspoon vanilla

1 teaspoon ground cinnamon

1/4teaspoon ground nutmeg

1/4 teaspoon ground ginger (optional)

Cashew Cream Icing

1 cup raw cashews

1/2 large lemon

2 tablespoons raw honey (or dried pitted dates)

1 teaspoon vanilla

Water

INSTRUCTIONS

1. *For *Cashew Cream Icing*, separately soak cashews and dates (if using) in enough water to cover for 2 hours. Drain dates. Drain and rinse cashews.

2. For *Carrot Cake*, add carrots to food processor or high-speed blender and pulse to roughly chop. Add all *Carrot Cake* ingredients and process until coarsely ground but still slightly chunky, about 1 minute.

3. Transfer mixture to cake or baking pan and press firmly with hands.

4. For *Cashew Cream Icing*, juice lemon and add to clean food processor or high-speed blender with soaked cashews, soaked dates or honey, and vanilla. Process until smooth, about 2 minutes. Add enough date soaking liquid or water to reach desired consistency.

5. Spread *Cashew Cream Icing* over *Carrot Cake* and place in refrigerator at least 2 hours.

6. Slice and serve chilled. Or allow to warm slightly and serve.

Amazing Chocolate Cake

Prep Time: 10 minutes*

Servings: 8

INGREDIENTS

Chocolate Cake

1 1/2 cups raw pecans

1 1/2 cups raw walnuts

1 1/2 cups dried pitted dates

1 1/2 cups raisins (or dried apricots or other dried fruit)

1/3 cup raw cocoa powder

2 teaspoons vanilla

Chocolate Icing

1 cup raw cashews

4 tablespoons raw honey (or dried pitted dates)

2 tablespoons raw cocoa powder

1/2 teaspoon vanilla

Water

INSTRUCTIONS

1. *For *Chocolate Icing*, separately soak cashews and dates (if using) in enough water to cover for 2 hours. Drain dates. Drain and rinse cashews.

2. For *Chocolate Cake*, add pecans and walnuts to food processor or high-speed blender. Process until coarsely ground, about 1 minute.

3. Add dates and process until finely ground, about 1 minute. Repeat with raisins, then cocoa and vanilla.

4. Process all ingredients until dough comes together. Transfer mixture to cake or baking pan and press firmly with hands.

5. For *Chocolate Icing*, add soaked cashews, soaked dates or honey, cocoa and vanilla to clean food processor or high-speed blender. Process until smooth, about 2 minutes. Add enough date soaking liquid or water to reach desired consistency.

6. Pour *Chocolate Icing* over *Chocolate Cake* and smooth with spatula or back of a spoon.

7. Refrigerate at least 1 hour, until cake is firm. Slice and serve chilled. Or allow to warm slightly and serve.

Paleo Red Velvet Cake

Prep Time: 15 minutes*

Servings: 8

INGREDIENTS

Red Velvet Cake

1 cup raw cashews

1 cup flaked or shredded coconut

1 cup dried pitted dates

4 beets (about 2 cups shredded)

1 large apple (or pear)

2 tablespoons raw coconut oil (or raw coconut or cacao butter, melted)

1 teaspoon vanilla

1/4 teaspoon Celtic sea salt

Cashew Frosting

1 cup raw cashews

1/3 cup dried pitted dates

2 tablespoons raw coconut oil (or raw coconut or cacao butter, melted)

1 teaspoon vanilla

Pinch Celtic sea salt

Water

INSTRUCTIONS

1. *For *Red Velvet Cake* and *Cashew Frosting*, separately soak cashews and dates in enough water to cover for 2 hours. Drain dates. Drain and rinse cashews.

2. For *Red Velvet Cake*, scrub and rinse beets. Remove roots and stems, and add to food processor or high-speed blender. Process to finely chop, about 2 minutes.

3. Peel and core apple. Add to processor and process to coarsely grind, about 1 minute.

4. Add coconut, soaked cashews and dates, coconut oil or butter, vanilla and salt. Process until mixture is finely ground and fairly smooth, up to 5 minutes.

5. Transfer mixture to cake or baking pan and press firmly with hands. Set aside in freezer.

6. For *Cashew Frosting*, add soaked cashews and dates, coconut oil or butter, vanilla and salt to clean food processor or high-speed blender. Process until smooth, about 2 minutes. Add enough date soaking liquid or water to reach desired consistency.

7. Spread *Cashew Frosting* over *Red Velvet Cake.*

8. Refrigerate or freeze at least 1 hour. Slice and serve chilled. Or allow to warm slightly and serve.

9. Store leftovers in freezer.

Paleo Plains Banana Bread

Prep Time: 10 minutes*

Dehydrating Time: 14 - 16 hours

Servings: 8

INGREDIENTS

Banana Bread

1 cup raw almonds

2 ripe bananas

2 sweet apples

2 carrots

1/2 cup flax meal (or flax seeds)

1/4 cup dried pitted dates

1/4 cup chopped walnuts

INSTRUCTIONS

1. Add whole flax to food processor or high-speed blender, if using. Process until finely ground, about 2 minutes.

2. Transfer flax meal to medium mixing bowl.

3. Add almonds to processor and process until finely ground, about 2 minutes. Add to flax.

4. Peel and core apples. Peel bananas. Roughly chop and add to processor. Process until puréed, about 2 minutes. Add to almond and flax meal.

5. Add carrots and dates to processor. Process until puréed, about 2 - 3 minutes. Add enough water to reached desired consistency, if necessary.

6. Add carrot and date purée to mixing bowl with walnuts. Mix to combine. Mixture should stick together. Add flax meal and/or water to reach desired consistency, if necessary.

7. Line dehydrator tray with dehydrator or parchment sheet.

8. Form mixture into loaves and place on lined dehydrator tray. Dehydrate at 118 degrees F for 14 - 16 hours. Until the outside is firm to the touch but the inside is still moist.

9. Remove from dehydrator and slice. Transfer to serving dish serve immediately. Or store in airtight container.

6. Add carrot and date purée to mixing bowl with walnuts. Mix to combine. Mixture should stick together. Add flax meal and/or water to reach desired consistency, if necessary.

7. Line dehydrator tray with dehydrator or parchment sheet.

8. Form mixture into loaves and place on lined dehydrator tray. Dehydrate at 118 degrees F for 14 - 16 hours. Until the outside is firm to the touch but the inside is still moist.

9. Remove from dehydrator and slice. Transfer to serving dish serve immediately. Or store in airtight container.

Paleo Plains Banana Bread

Prep Time: 10 minutes*

Dehydrating Time: 14 - 16 hours

Servings: 8

INGREDIENTS

Banana Bread

1 cup raw almonds

2 ripe bananas

2 sweet apples

2 carrots

1/2 cup flax meal (or flax seeds)

1/4 cup dried pitted dates

1/4 cup chopped walnuts

INSTRUCTIONS

1. Add whole flax to food processor or high-speed blender, if using. Process until finely ground, about 2 minutes.
2. Transfer flax meal to medium mixing bowl.
3. Add almonds to processor and process until finely ground, about 2 minutes. Add to flax.
4. Peel and core apples. Peel bananas. Roughly chop and add to processor. Process until puréed, about 2 minutes. Add to almond and flax meal.
5. Add carrots and dates to processor. Process until puréed, about 2 - 3 minutes. Add enough water to reached desired consistency, if necessary.

Moist Coconut Macaroons

Prep Time: 15 minutes

Dehydrating Time: 24 hours

Servings: 12

INGREDIENTS

2 1/2 cups flaked or shredded coconut

1/3 cup dried pitted dates

1/3 cup water

1/2 teaspoon vanilla

Pinch Celtic sea salt

INSTRUCTIONS

2. Add 1 1/4 cups coconut to food processor or high-speed blender. Process until smooth and creamy, up to 5 minutes. Scrape down sides of bowl as necessary.

3. Add dates, water, vanilla and salt to processor. Process until smooth, about 2 minutes.

4. Transfer mixture to medium mixing bowl. Add remaining coconut and mix until well combined.

5. Line dehydrator tray with dehydrator or parchment sheets.

6. Use scoop or tablespoon to drop cookies onto lined dehydrator trays. Dehydrate at 118 degrees F for about 24 hours. Until the outside is dry to the touch but the inside is still moist.

7. Remove from dehydrator and transfer to serving dish. Serve immediately. Or store in airtight container.

Delicious Chocolate Chip Cookies

Prep Time: 20 minutes*

Dehydrating Time: 6 - 12 hours

Servings: 12

INGREDIENTS

2 cups raw cashew flour (or 3 cups raw cashews)

1 cup almond butter (or 1 1/2 cups raw almonds)

2 tablespoons raw coconut oil (or raw coconut or cacao butter, melted)

1 tablespoon flax meal

3/4 cup dried pitted dates

2 teaspoons vanilla

1 teaspoon Celtic sea salt

1 cup raw chocolate chips (or cacao nibs or raw chocolate bark)

Water

INSTRUCTIONS

1. *Soak dates in enough water to cover for at least 6 hours, or overnight in refrigerator. Drain, reserving soaking liquid.
2. Add cashews to food processor or high-speed blender. Process until finely ground, about 2 minutes. Transfer cashew flour to medium mixing bowl.
3. Add almonds (if using) to processor and process until smooth and creamy, up to 8 minutes. Scrape down as necessary.
4. Add dates, coconut oil or butter, flax, vanilla and salt to almond butter in processor. Process until smooth, about 1 - 2 minutes. Transfer mixture to mixing bowl.

5. Chop raw chocolate bark, if using. Add cacao nibs or raw chocolate and mix well to combine. Add date soaking liquid to reach desired consistency. Dough should be moist and stick together.
6. Line dehydrator trays with dehydrator or parchment sheets.
7. Form mixture into balls and place on dehydrator or parchment sheets. Press to flatten.
8. Place in dehydrator and dehydrate at 118 degrees F for about 6 - 12 hours, depending on desired crispiness. Outside should be firm while inside is still moist.
9. Remove from dehydrator and transfer to serving dish. Serve immediately. Or store in airtight container.

All-American Almond Biscotti

Prep Time: 10 minutes*

Dehydrating Time: 12 - 24 hours

Servings: 12

INGREDIENTS

1 1/2 cups raw almond flour

2 cups raw almonds

1 cup flaked or shredded coconut

1/2 cup raw honey (or dried pitted dates)

1/2 cup dried apricots or golden raisins (optional)

1 teaspoon vanilla

1/4 teaspoon Celtic sea salt

Water

INSTRUCTIONS

1. *Soak dates in enough water to cover overnight in refrigerator, if using. Drain, reserving soaking liquid.

2. Add 1 1/2 cups almonds to food processor or high-speed blender. Process until finely ground, about 2 minutes.

3. Add coconut to processor and process until finely ground, about 1 minute.

4. Add soaked dates or honey, vanilla, salt, and apricots or raisins (optional) to processor. Process until well ground, about 1 - 2 minutes. Transfer mixture to mixing bowl.

5. Add almond flour and remaining 1/2 cup raw almonds. Mix well to combine. Add date soaking liquid to reach desired consistency. Dough should be moist and stick together.
6. Line dehydrator trays with dehydrator or parchment sheets.
7. Form mixture into loaves and place on dehydrator or parchment sheets.
8. Place in dehydrator and dehydrate at 118 degrees F for about 8 hours.
9. Remove from dehydrator and cut into 3/4 inch slices. Turn slices on sides and place directly on dehydrator tray. Continue dehydrating 4 - 16 hours, depending on desired crispiness.
10. Remove from dehydrator and transfer to serving dish. Serve immediately. Or store in airtight container.

Simple Ginger Pudding

Prep Time: 20 minutes*

Servings: 2

INGREDIENTS

1 young coconut (about 1 cup coconut meat and 1 cup coconut water)

2 - 4 tablespoons raw honey (or pitted dates)

1 1/2 inch piece fresh ginger

1/2 teaspoon ground ginger

1 teaspoon vanilla

Water (optional)

INSTRUCTIONS

1. * Soak dates in enough water to cover for at least 4 hours, or overnight in refrigerator (if using). Drain.

2. Remove flesh from fresh coconut and add to high-speed blender with 1 cup coconut water. Process until well blended and fairly smooth, about 1 - 2 minutes.

3. Peel ginger and grate into processor. Add vanilla, ground ginger, and honey or dates. Process until smooth, about 1 minute.

4. Transfer to serving dish and serve immediately or refrigerate at least 20 minutes and serve chilled.

Primal Strawberry Ice Cream

Prep Time: 30 minutes

Servings: 4

INGREDIENTS

2 coconuts (or 1 cup flaked coconut)

2 tablespoons raw honey (or dried pitted dates)

2 cup strawberries (fresh or thawed)

1/2 teaspoon vanilla

Water

INSTRUCTIONS

1. *Freeze ice cream maker canister for overnight.
2. *Soak flaked coconut and dates in 2 cups water overnight in refrigerator, if using.
3. Add soaked coconut and dates, plus soaking liquid to high-speed blender. Process until well blended and fairly smooth, about 1 - 2 minutes.
4. Or remove flesh from fresh coconuts and add to high-speed blender with 2 cups water. Process until well blended and fairly smooth, about 1 - 2 minutes.
5. Strain mixture through nut milk bag, cheesecloth or strainer back into blender.
6. Reserve pulp and set aside to dry and dehydrate, then use as coconut flour.

7. Remove stems from strawberries, then cut in half. Add to blender with honey or dates, and vanilla. Process until smooth, about 1 minute.

8. Turn on ice cream maker. Slowly pour mixture into running ice cream maker. Let machine run until ice cream forms, about 20 minutes.

9. Transfer to serving dish and serve immediately. Or store in airtight container in freezer.

Coconut Mango Sorbet

Prep Time: 30 minutes

Servings: 4

INGREDIENTS

2 coconuts (or 1 cup flaked coconut)

3 ripe mangos

1 orange

INSTRUCTIONS

1. *Freeze ice cream maker canister overnight.
2. *Soak flaked coconut in 2 cups water overnight in refrigerator, if using.
3. Add soaked coconut and soaking liquid to high-speed blender. Process until well blended and fairly smooth, about 1 - 2 minutes.
4. Or remove flesh from fresh coconuts and add to high-speed blender with 2 cups water. Process until well blended and fairly smooth, about 1 - 2 minutes.
5. Strain mixture through nut milk bag, cheesecloth or strainer back into blender.
6. Reserve pulp and set aside to dry and dehydrate, then use as coconut flour.
7. Cut mangos in half and remove peel. Roughly chop and add to blender. Zest *then* juice orange. Add to processor and process until smooth, about 1 minute.

8. Turn on ice cream maker. Slowly pour mixture into running ice cream maker. Let machine run until ice cream forms, about 20 minutes.
9. Transfer to serving dish and serve immediately. Or store in airtight container in freezer.

Snack Recipes

Introduction

Welcome to the guide for followers of the Paleo diet out there who are in need of some delicious and nutritious snacks. This book can really help anyone who wants some healthy snack ideas for themselves and their family. We all know that snacks can be an easy way to fall from a healthy diet plan. It is easy and convenient to pick up processed, refined and affordable snacks. Not to mention when our blood sugar levels drop, those unhealthy snacks start to sound even better. Fear not, with this recipe book you can be prepared. Choose from a large variety of flavors and combinations.

When eating like our Paleolithic ancestors, all ingredients are natural and have no refined sugars or processing. These recipes combine the whole ingredients in ways our ancestors couldn't have even imagined! Enjoy delicious combinations like hazelnut spread on apples and cherry pie bars. Who said eating healthy couldn't be indulgent as well? Nature has provided sweets that are also packed with nutrition. So, go ahead and keep walking past that vending machine full of cookies and candy bars. Prepare your snacks at the beginning of the week and enjoy delicious snacks at home or on the go.

Table of Contents

Primal Almond Crunch Cookies

Primal Ginger Cookies

Cocoa Coated Almonds

Paleo Cocoa Chia Pudding

Paleo Rice Pudding

Nori and Almond Cheese Snacks

Paleo Asian Slaw

Sweet Strawberry Salsa

Tropical Mango Salsa

Spicy Pineapple Apricot Salsa

Real Deal Pico de Gallo

Paleo Loaded Guacamole

Stuffed Jalapeño Bites

Primal Sesame Crackers

Prep Time: 10 minutes

Dehydrating Time: 12 - 20 hours

Servings: 4

INGREDIENTS

2 cups ground flax seed

2/3 cup whole flax seed

1 1/3 cups raw sunflower seeds

1/2 cup raw black sesame seeds (or white sesame seeds)

Small bunch fresh parsley

1/4 teaspoon dried basil

1/4 teaspoon onion powder

1/4 teaspoon garlic powder

1 teaspoon Celtic sea salt

2 2/3 cups water

INSTRUCTIONS

1. Place parchment paper or dehydrator sheets on two dehydrator trays.
2. Finely mince fresh parsley. Add to large mixing bowl with seeds, salt and spices. Mix until well combined.
3. Spread batter on prepared sheets. Place trays in dehydrator and set to 120 degrees F for 1 hour. Reduce temperature to 105 degrees F for remainder of dehydrating time.

4. After 4 hours dehydrating time, remove trays from dehydrator and use knife to score crackers in preferred shape and size. Place back in dehydrator and continue dehydrating another 4 hours.

5. Remove trays from dehydrator. Peel crackers from sheets and break apart along score lines. Place crackers directly on dehydrator tray and continue dehydrating another 4 - 12 hours, depending on desired crispness.

6. Remove crackers from dehydrator and serve with your favorite raw dips, spreads and salsas. Or store in an airtight container up to 4 weeks.

Simple Veggie Crackers

Prep Time: 10 minutes

Cook Time: 12 - 24 hours

Servings: 4

INGREDIENTS

1 medium tomato

1 medium onion

2 medium zucchini

1 cup ground flax seed

2 tablespoons coconut aminos (or raw apple cider vinegar)

1/2 teaspoon ground black pepper

1 teaspoon Celtic sea salt

INSTRUCTIONS

1. Place parchment paper or dehydrator sheets on two dehydrator trays.
2. Peel onion and chop. Chop zucchini and tomato. Add to food processor or high-speed blender with flax meal, coconut aminos or vinegar, salt and pepper. Process until well ground, about 2 minutes.
3. Spread batter on prepared sheets. Place trays in dehydrator and set to 120 degrees F for 1 hour. Reduce temperature to 105 degrees F for remainder of dehydrating time.
4. After 4 hours dehydrating time, remove trays from dehydrator and use knife to score crackers in preferred shape and size. Place back in dehydrator and continue dehydrating another 4 hours.

5. Remove trays from dehydrator. Peel crackers from sheets and break apart along score lines. Place crackers directly on dehydrator tray and continue dehydrating another 4 - 12 hours, depending on desired crispness.

6. Remove crackers from dehydrator and serve with your favorite raw dips, spreads and salsas. Or store in an airtight container up to 4 weeks.

Primal Avocado Hummus with Cucumber Chips

Prep Time: 5 minutes*

Servings: 4

INGREDIENTS

1 cup raw cashews

1 avocado

Juice of 1/2 lemon

2 garlic cloves

1 teaspoon ground white pepper (or 1/2 teaspoon ground black pepper)

Small bunch fresh cilantro

1/2 teaspoon Celtic sea salt

1 small cucumber

Water

INSTRUCTIONS

1. *Soak cashews in enough water to cover at least 4 hours, or overnight in refrigerator. Drain and rinse.
2. Peel garlic. Juice lemon. Remove cilantro leaves from stem. Add to food processor or high-speed blender with soaked cashews, salt and pepper.
3. Slice avocado in half. Remove pit and scoop flesh into processor. Process until smooth, about 1 - 2 minutes. Add water or raw oil to reach desired consistency, if necessary.
4. Transfer mixture to serving dish.

5. Peel cucumber if desired. Cut diagonally into 1/3 inch slices. Arrange on serving dish.

6. Serve immediately with hummus. Or place in refrigerator for 20 minutes, then serve chilled.

Paleo Mediterranean Hummus with Carrots

Prep Time: 5 minutes*

Servings: 4

INGREDIENTS

1 1/2 cup raw cashews

1/4 cup sundried tomatoes

1/4 cup raw tahini (or 1/3 cup raw sesame seeds)

1/2 lemon

1 small garlic clove

1 teaspoon ground white pepper (or 1/2 teaspoon ground black pepper)

1/2 teaspoon Celtic sea salt

2 large carrots

Water

INSTRUCTIONS

1. *Soak cashews in enough water to cover at least 4 hours, or overnight in refrigerator. Drain and rinse.
2. Peel garlic. Juice lemon. Add to food processor or high-speed blender with raw sesame seeds and process until smooth, if using.
3. Or add tahini to processor with soaked cashews, sundried tomatoes, garlic, lemon juice, salt and pepper. Process until smooth, about 1 - 2 minutes. Add water or raw oil to reach desired consistency, if necessary.
4. Transfer mixture to serving dish.

7. Peel carrots if desired. Cut into 4 inch long x 1/2 inch thick sticks. Arrange on serving dish.

5. Serve immediately with hummus. Or place in refrigerator for 20 minutes, then serve chilled.

Simple Chocolate Date Spread

Prep Time: 5 minutes*

Servings: 4

INGREDIENTS

10 - 12 oz dried pitted dates

2 cups water

3 tablespoons raw cocoa powder

1/2 teaspoon ground cinnamon

1/4 teaspoon ground ginger

Ground black pepper, to taste

INSTRUCTIONS

1. *Soak dates in water overnight. Drain and reserve 1/4 cup liquid.

2. Add soaked dates, cocoa powder, cinnamon, ginger and black pepper to taste to food processor or high-speed blender. Pulse until chunky mixture forms. Add reserved liquid to reach desired consistency, if necessary.

3. Or add dates to medium mixing bowl with cocoa powder, cinnamon, ginger and black pepper to taste. Mash with large fork or potato masher for about 5 minutes, until chunky mixture forms. Add reserved liquid to reach desired consistency, if necessary.

4. Transfer to serving dish and serve with fruits, veggies, or raw crackers and breads.

Primal Spinach Dip with Pepper Chips

Prep Time: 10 minutes

Servings: 2

INGREDIENTS

2 - 3 cups spinach leaves

1 1/2 cups raw cashews

3 garlic cloves

1 lemon

1/3 cup water

1/4 teaspoon mustard powder (or mustard seeds)

1/2 teaspoon ground white pepper (or 1/4 teaspoon ground black pepper)

1/2 teaspoon Celtic sea salt

1 red bell pepper

INSTRUCTIONS

1. Cut bell pepper in half and remove seeds, veins and stems. Slice peppers into 1 - 1 1/2 inch strips. Arrange on serving dish and set aside.

2. Juice lemon. Peel garlic. Add to food processor or high-speed blender with cashews and mustard powder or seeds. Process until finely ground, about 2 minutes.

3. Add salt, pepper and water. Process until smooth. Add spinach and pulse until spinach is desired texture.

4. Transfer mixture to serving dish. Serving immediately with bell pepper slices. Or refrigerate 20 minutes and serve chilled.

Paleo Hazelnut Spread with Apples

Prep Time: 5 minutes*

Servings: 2

INGREDIENTS

1 cup raw hazelnuts

1/4 cup raw cocoa powder

1/4 cup raw honey (or dried pitted dates)

2/3 teaspoon vanilla

1/4 teaspoon Celtic sea salt

2 apples

Raw nut milk (optional)

Water

INSTRUCTIONS

1. *Soak hazelnuts in enough water to cover overnight in refrigerator. Soak dates in enough water to cover overnight in refrigerator, if using. Drain and rinse.

2. Add soaked hazelnuts to food processor or high-speed blender and process until smooth, up to 10 minutes. Scrape down sides as needed.

3. Add honey or soaked dates, cocoa powder, vanilla and salt. Process until smooth, about 1 minute. Add nut milk to reach desired consistency, if necessary.

4. Transfer mixture to serving dish.

5. Remove core, seeds and stems from apples. Slice into wedges and arrange on serving dish. Serve immediately.

Cashew Butter Stuffed Dates

Prep Time: 5 minutes

Servings: 2

INGREDIENTS

6 whole dried pitted dates

Pinch ground cinnamon

Raw Cashew Butter

1 cup raw cashews

1 dried pitted date

1 teaspoon raw oil (coconut, walnut, almond, sesame, etc.)

1/2 teaspoon ground cinnamon

1/4 teaspoon Celtic sea salt

(or 1/2 cup prepared raw cashew butter)

INSTRUCTIONS

1. For *Cashew Butter*, add cashews, date, cinnamon, salt and oil to food processor or high-speed blender. Process until smooth, up to 5 minutes. Let mixture rest between periods of processing to reach desired consistency, if necessary.
2. Slice dates in half lengthwise. Use small spoon to fill date halves with prepared or *Raw Cashew Butter*. Sprinkle ground cinnamon over filled dates.
3. Arrange on serving dish and serve immediately.

Paleo Cherry Pie Bars

Prep Time: 25 minutes

Servings: 6

INGREDIENTS

1 cup dried cherries

1/4 cup dried pitted dates

1 cup raw almonds

1/4 teaspoon ground cinnamon

1/4 teaspoon vanilla

1/8 teaspoon Celtic sea salt

1/3 cup warm water

1/2 sour orange (or orange or tangerine)

INSTRUCTIONS

1. Zest and juice orange into small mixing bowl. Add warm water and dried cherries. Toss to coat and set aside 10 minutes.
2. Line loaf pan with parchment paper.
3. Add nuts and dates to food processor or high-speed blender. Drain soaked cherries and add to processor with cinnamon, vanilla and salt. Process for about 1 minute, until mixture is coarsely ground and sticks together when pressed.
4. Scrape mixture into prepared loaf pan and press firmly into bottom with hands or spatula.
5. Place in refrigerator and chill for 10 minutes. Remove and cut into 6 bars.
6. Serve immediately. Or store in refrigerator up to 2 weeks.

Paleo Coconut Ambrosia Salad

Prep Time: 15 minutes*

Servings: 2

INGREDIENTS

3 mature coconuts

1 1/2 cups water

6 clementines or tangerines (about 1 cup segments)

1 cup fresh pineapple (chopped)

1 cup pecans (chopped)

1 cup fresh cherries (pitted)

INSTRUCTIONS

5. Remove coconut flesh from shells. Add 1 coconut and water to food processor or high-speed blender. Process until well blended and fairly smooth, about 1 - 2 minutes.

6. Strain mixture through nut milk bag, cheesecloth or strainer into container. Add coconut milk back to blender with flesh of 2nd coconut. Process again until well blended and thick, about 1 - 2 minutes.

7. Strain mixture through nut milk bag, cheesecloth or strainer into container. Reserve pulp and set aside to dry and dehydrate, then use as coconut flour.

8. *For thicker coconut cream, set aside thickened milk in refrigerator about 20 minutes and allow fat to separate. Remove coconut cream from refrigerator and scoop out risen fat into medium mixing bowl.

9. Or add coconut cream milk to medium mixing bowl. Peel oranges or tangerines and remove segments. Peel pineapple and chop. Cut cherries in half and pit. Chop pecans. Add to coconut cream.

10. Add remaining coconut flesh to clean food processor with shredding attachment and process, or grate with grater. Add coconut to mixture. Stir to combine.

11. Cover mixture and place in refrigerator for 2 hours. Remove and transfer to serving dishes.

12. Serve chilled.

Paleo Carrot Raisin Salad

Prep Time: 5 minutes

Servings: 2

INSTRUCTIONS

2 large carrots

2 tablespoons red raisins

2 tablespoons golden raisins

1/4 cup raw slivered almonds (or sliced almonds)

1/2 small orange (or tangerine)

1/4 teaspoon ground cinnamon

DIRECTIONS

1. Add carrots to food processor with shredding attachment and process, or grate with grater. Add to medium mixing bowl with raisins, almonds and cinnamon.
2. Zest *then* juice orange. Add to carrot mixture and toss to combine.
3. Transfer to serving dishes and serve immediately. Or refrigerate 20 minutes and serve chilled.

Paleo Sticky Rice with Mango

Prep Time: 10 minutes*

Servings: 2

INSTRUCTIONS

1 fresh coconut (or 2/3 cup desiccated, shredded or flaked coconut)

1/4 cup raw honey (or 1/4 cup dried pitted dates)

1/4 teaspoon ground ginger(or 1/4 inch piece fresh ginger)

1 mango

INGREDIENTS

1. *Soak dried coconut and dried pitted dates in enough water to cover overnight in refrigerator, if using. Drain coconut and add to medium mixing bowl. Drain dates and reserve 2 tablespoons soaking liquid.

2. Or remove fresh coconut flesh from shell and add to food processor with shredding attachment and process, or grate with grater. Add to medium mixing bowl.

3. Add soaked dates and soaking liquid to clean food processor or high-speed and process until smooth, if using.

4. Peel fresh ginger and mince or finely grate, if using. Add raw honey or date purée to shredded coconut with ground or fresh ginger. Mix to combine. Transfer to serving dishes.

5. Slice mango in half around pit. Remove peel and dice or thinly slice flesh. Add over sweet shredded coconut.

6. Serve immediately. Or refrigerate 20 minutes and serve chilled.

Primal Almond Crunch Cookies

Prep Time: 20 minutes

Servings: 12

INGREDIENTS

3/4 cup raw almond butter (or 1 cup raw almonds)

2 - 4 tablespoons raw honey (or 1/4 cup dried pitted dates)

1 tablespoon ground chia seed or flax meal (or whole seeds)

1 teaspoon cinnamon

1/2 teaspoon Celtic sea salt

1/4 cup raw almonds

INSTRUCTIONS

1. Line baking dish with parchment paper.
2. Add 1/4 cup raw almonds to food processor or high-speed blender and process until finely chopped. Set aside.
3. Add whole chia or flax seeds to high-speed blender or spice grinder and grind to fine powder, if using.
4. Add chia or flax meal to food processor or high-speed blender with remaining almonds or almond butter, honey or dates, cinnamon and salt. Process until smooth, thick paste forms, up to 5 minutes. Let mixture rest between periods of processing to reach desired consistency, if necessary.
5. Spread mixture in parchment lined dish. Place in refrigerator or freezer for 10 minutes.
6. Remove dish and scoop with tablespoon or melon baller. Roll into balls with hands.

7. Place chopped almonds in shallow dish and roll balls in almonds to coat.

8. Transfer coated almond cookies to serving dish. Serve immediately. Or refrigerate 20 minutes and serve chilled.

Primal Ginger Cookies

Prep Time: 20 minutes*

Servings: 12

INGREDIENTS

1/2 cup raw cashews (frozen)

1 1/2 cups dried pitted dates (1 cup chopped)

2 inch piece fresh ginger

1 teaspoon ground ginger

1/4 teaspoon ground cinnamon

1/2 cup unsweetened flaked or shredded coconut

INSTRUCTIONS

5. * Place cashews in freezer for a few hours to overnight.

6. Add frozen nuts to food processor or high-speed blender. Pulse until coarsely ground.

7. Peel and finely grate fresh ginger. Add to processor with dates, ground ginger and cinnamon. Process until mixture is well broken down and sticks together.

8. Form mixture into 12 balls. Add coconut flakes to shallow dish. Roll balla in coconut until well coated, then gently press to flatten slightly.

9. Arrange on serving dish and cover. Place in freezer for at least 10 minutes, until set up and firm.

10. Remove from freezer and serve chilled. Or store in freezer or refrigerator.

Cocoa Coated Almonds

Prep Time: 20 minutes*

Servings: 2

INGREDIENTS

1 cup raw almonds

1 tablespoon raw cocoa powder

1 tablespoon raw honey

1/8 teaspoon ground cinnamon

1/8 teaspoon vanilla

INSTRUCTIONS

1. Add almonds and honey to small mixing bowl and toss to combine.
2. Add cocoa, cinnamon and vanilla and toss to evenly coat.
3. Transfer to serving dish and serve immediately.

Paleo Cocoa Chia Pudding

Prep Time: 15 minutes

Servings: 2

INGREDIENTS

1 cup nut milk (or 2 mature coconuts + 1 1/2 cups water)

2 - 4 tablespoons raw honey (or dried pitted dates)

2 - 4 tablespoons whole chia seeds

2 - 3 tablespoons cocoa powder

1/2 teaspoon vanilla

INSTRUCTIONS

1. Remove coconut flesh from shells. Add 1 coconut and water to food processor or high-speed blender. Process until well blended and fairly smooth, about 1- 2 minutes.

2. Strain mixture through nut milk bag, cheesecloth or strainer into container. Add coconut milk back to blender with remaining coconut flesh. Process again until well blended and fairly smooth, about 1 minute.

3. Strain mixture through nut milk bag, cheesecloth or strainer into container. Reserve pulp and set aside to dry and dehydrate, then use as coconut flour.

4. Add nut milk to high-speed blender with dates and process until smooth, if using.

5. Or add nut milk to small mixing bowl with honey or stevia, cocoa powder, vanilla and chia seeds. Whisk to combine. Set aside to thicken, about 1 minute.

6. Pour mixture into serving dishes and serve immediately. Or refrigerate 20 minutes and serve chilled.

Paleo Rice Pudding

Prep Time: 20 minutes

Servings: 4

INGREDIENTS

3 fresh coconuts (or 2 cups unsweetened flaked or shredded coconut)

1 cup water

1/4 - 1/2 cup raw honey (or dried pitted dates)

1 teaspoon vanilla

Water

INSTRUCTIONS

1. *Soak 1 1/2 cups flaked coconut and dates in enough water to cover in refrigerator overnight. Then drain, if using.
2. Or remove fresh coconut flesh from shells.
3. Add flesh of 1 fresh coconut or 3/4 cup soaked coconut, and water to high-speed blender. Process until well blended and fairly smooth, about 1- 2 minutes.
4. Strain mixture through nut milk bag, cheesecloth or strainer into container. Add coconut milk back to blender with flesh of 1 fresh coconut or remaining soaked coconut. Process again until well blended and fairly smooth, about 1 minute.
5. Strain mixture through nut milk bag, cheesecloth or strainer into container. Reserve pulp and set aside to dry and dehydrate, then use as coconut flour.
6. Add coconut cream, soaked dates and vanilla to food processor or high-speed blender. Process until smooth, about 1 minute.

7. Or add coconut cream to medium mixing bowl with raw honey and vanilla.
8. Add remaining fresh coconut flesh to food processer with shredding attachment and process, or shred with grater.
9. Add shredded fresh coconut or flaked coconut to coconut cream mixture and whisk until well combined.
10. Pour into serving dishes and serve immediately. Or refrigerate for 20 minutes and serve chilled.

Nori and Almond Cheese Snacks

Prep Time: 15 minutes*

Servings: 2

INGREDIENTS

4 - 6 sheets dried nori (seaweed paper)

Almond cheese

1 cup raw almonds

2 tablespoons raw oil (coconut, walnut, almond, sesame, etc.)

2 tablespoons lemon juice (or raw apple cider vinegar)

1 garlic clove

1/4 teaspoon paprika

1/4 teaspoon ground white pepper (or ground black pepper)

1/2 teaspoon Celtic sea salt

Water

INSTRUCTIONS

1. *For *Almond Cheese*, soak almonds in enough water to cover overnight. Drain and rinse. Pop off skins and discard.
2. Peel garlic and add to food processor or high-speed blender with soaked almonds, oil, lemon juice and/or vinegar, salt and spices. Process until smooth, about 2 minutes. Add water to reach desired consistency, if necessary.
3. Transfer mixture to small serving dish. Cut nori into small sheets and arrange on serving dish.
4. Serve immediately. Or refrigerate for 20 minutes and serve chilled.

Paleo Asian Slaw

Prep Time: 15 minutes*

Servings: 4

INGREDIENTS

1/2 head red cabbage (2 cups shredded)

2 broccoli stalks (2 cups shredded)

1/4 cup dried cranberries

1/4 cup raw sliced or slivered almonds

2 tablespoons raw sunflower seeds

2 green onions (scallions)

1 carrot

1 lemon

1/2 orange

2 tablespoons raw honey

2 tablespoons raw sesame oil (or coconut, walnut, almond oil, etc.)

2 tablespoons apple cider vinegar

1/2 teaspoon ground ginger

1 teaspoon ground white pepper (or black pepper)

1 teaspoon Celtic sea salt

INSTRUCTIONS

1. Add broccoli and carrot to food processor with shredding attachment, or grate with grater. Slice green onions. Shred cabbage. Add to large mixing bowl.

2. Add cranberries, almonds, sunflower seeds, honey, oil, vinegar, ginger, salt, pepper and squeeze of lemon and orange. Mix until well combined.

3. *Transfer mixture and for 90 minutes. Serve chilled.

Sweet Strawberry Salsa

Prep Time: 5 minutes*

Servings: 4

INGREDIENTS

2 cups fresh strawberries

1/2 small white onion

1/4 red bell pepper

Medium bunch fresh mint

1/2 lime

1/2 orange

1/2 teaspoon ground black pepper

INSTRUCTIONS

1. Remove strawberry stems and leaves, then finely dice. Add to medium mixing bowl.
2. Peel onion and finely dice. Remove mint leave s from stem then chiffon, or thinly slice. Add to strawberries with pepper and squeeze of lime and orange. Mix until well combined.
3. Transfer mixture to serving dish and serve immediately with raw chips. Or refrigerate for 20 minutes and serve chilled.

Tropical Mango Salsa

Prep Time: 10 minutes

Servings: 4

INGREDIENTS

2 mangos

1/4 small red onion

1/4 red bell pepper

Small bunch fresh cilantro

1 lime

1/2 fresh jalapeño pepper

1/4 teaspoon Celtic sea salt

INSTRUCTIONS

1. Slice mangos in half around pit. Remove peel and finely dice flesh. Add to medium mixing bowl.

2. Peel onion and dice. Remove seeds, stem and vein from bell pepper, then finely dice. Finely chop cilantro. Remove seeds and stem from jalapeño, then mince. Add to mango with salt and squeeze of lime. Mix until well combined

3. Transfer mixture to serving dish and serve immediately with raw chips. Or refrigerate for 20 minutes and serve chilled.

Spicy Pineapple Apricot Salsa

Prep Time: 15 minutes

Servings: 4

INGREDIENTS

1 cup fresh pineapple (diced)

3 fresh apricots

1/2 green bell pepper

1/2 cup cherry tomatoes

2 shallots

2 garlic cloves

1 lime

1 fresh Serrano pepper

Small bunch cilantro leaves

1/2 teaspoon cayenne pepper

1/4 teaspoon Celtic sea salt

INSTRUCTIONS

1. Peel pineapple and finely dice. Cut apricots in half and remove pits, then finely dice. Add to medium mixing bowl.
2. Peel shallots and thinly slice. Peel garlic and mince or thinly slice. Remove seeds, stem and vein from bell pepper, then finely dice. Quarter cherry tomatoes. Add to pineapple and apricot.
3. Finely chop cilantro. Remove seeds and stem from Serrano pepper, then mince. Add to bowl with salt, cayenne and squeeze of lime. Mix until well combined.

4. Transfer mixture to serving dish and serve immediately with raw chips. Or refrigerate for 20 minutes and serve chilled.

Real Deal Pico de Gallo

Prep Time: 15 minutes*

Servings: 4

INGREDIENTS

4 plum tomatoes

1/2 small red onion

Small bunch fresh cilantro

1/2 jalapeño pepper

1/2 lime

1 garlic clove

1/8 teaspoon garlic powder

1/4 teaspoon ground cumin

1/4 teaspoon Celtic sea salt

1/4 teaspoon ground black pepper

INSTRUCTIONS

1. Finely dice tomatoes. Peel and dice onion. Add to medium mixing bowl.
2. Finely chop cilantro. Remove seeds, veins and stem from jalapeño, then mince. Peel and mince garlic. Add to tomatoes with salt, spices and squeeze of lime. Mix until well combined.
3. Transfer mixture to serving dish
4. *Refrigerate 3 hours. Serve room temperature or chilled with raw chips.

Paleo Loaded Guacamole

Prep Time: 5 minutes

Servings: 2

INGREDIENTS

2 ripe avocados

1 small plum tomato

1/4 small red onion

Medium bunch fresh cilantro

1/2 lime

1/2 teaspoon smoked paprika

1/2 teaspoon ground black pepper

1/2 teaspoon Celtic sea salt

INSTRUCTIONS

1. Cut avocados in half and remove pits. Scoop flesh into small mixing bowl.
2. Peel onion and dice. Dice tomato. Finely chop cilantro. Add to avocado with salt, spices, and squeeze of lime. Mash with fork until well combined.
3. Transfer mixture to serving dish and serve immediately with raw chips. Or refrigerate for 20 minutes and serve chilled.

Stuffed Jalapeño Bites

Prep Time: 15 minutes*

Dehydrating Time: 8 - 24 hours

Servings: 4

INGREDIENTS

6 fresh jalapeño peppers

1 cup raw sunflower seeds

1/2 cup water

1/4 cup nutritional yeast

1 lemon

2 teaspoons onion powder

1/2 teaspoon cayenne pepper

1 teaspoon Celtic sea salt

Water

INSTRUCTIONS

1. *Soak sunflower seeds in enough water to cover for 2 hours. Drain and rinse.

2. Cut jalapeños in half lengthwise and remove stems, seeds and veins. Place peppers on dehydrator tray.

3. Juice lemon. Add to food processor or high-speed blender with soaked sunflower seeds, water, nutritional yeast, salt, pepper and spices. Process until thick, smooth paste forms, about 2 minutes.

4. Fill piping bag with mixture and pipe into jalapeño halves. Or use teaspoon to scoop filling into jalapeño halves.

5. Place stuffed peppers on dehydrator sheets filling-side up. Set dehydrator to 110 degrees F for 8 - 24 hours, depending on desired texture.

6. Remove peppers from dehydrator and serve immediately.

6170414R00073

Printed in Great Britain
by Amazon.co.uk, Ltd.,
Marston Gate.